First Facts™

Everyday Character Education

Consideration

by Sarah L. Schuette

Consultant:
Madonna Murphy, PhD, Professor of Education
University of St. Francis, Joliet, Illinois
Author, *Character Education in America's Blue Ribbon Schools*

Capstone *press*

Mankato, Minnesota

First Facts is published by Capstone Press,
151 Good Counsel Drive, P.O. Box 669, Mankato, Minnesota 56002.
www.capstonepress.com

Library of Congress Cataloging-in-Publication Data
Schuette, Sarah L., 1976–
    Consideration / by Sarah L. Schuette.
    p. cm. — (First facts. Everyday character education)
    Includes bibliographical references and index.
    ISBN 0-7368-3677-2 (hardcover)
    1. Thoughtfulness—Juvenile literature. I. Title. II. Series.
BJ1533.T45.S38 2005
177'.7—dc22   2004012797

Summary: Introduces consideration through examples of everyday situations where
this character trait can be used.

Editorial Credits
Wendy Dieker, editor; Molly Nei, set designer; Kia Adams, book designer;
    Jo Miller, photo researcher

Photo Credits
Capstone Press/Karon Dubke, cover, 6–7
Corbis/Reuters, 20
Gem Photo Studio/Dan Delaney, 1, 5, 8, 9, 11, 12, 13, 19
Getty Images Inc./John Chillingworth, 16–17
Photo courtesy of Dee Leanna/Heavenly Hats Foundation, 15

The author dedicates this book to the memory of her friend Carol Vinkemeier of Stewart, Minnesota.

1 2 3 4 5 6 10 09 08 07 06 05

Table of Contents

Consideration 4

At Your School 7

With Your Friends 8

At Home 10

In Your Community 12

Anthony Leanna 14

C. S. Lewis 16

What Would You Do? 18

Amazing but True! 20
Hands On: Give Thank-You Notes 21
Glossary 22
Read More 23
Internet Sites 23
Index 24

Consideration

Lexi raises her hand to answer her teacher's question. But Jacob raised his hand first. Lexi does not shout out the answer. She knows Jacob would feel bad if he didn't get a chance to answer. Lexi shows consideration by thinking about Jacob's feelings before her own.

Fact!
A good way to be considerate is to treat people in a way that you would like to be treated.

At Your School

School is a good place to show consideration. You can help a classmate pick up the papers she dropped. Your teacher will like the good **example** that you set. School is fun when everyone is considerate.

With Your Friends

Being considerate shows your friends that you care about them. Be on time if a friend invites you to her home.

You can let your friend choose a
game to play. When it is time to leave,
thank her for inviting you to her home.

At Home

Think about the needs of the people in your family. Help your dad put away the groceries.

Maybe your mom is tired after a long day at work. Offer to set the table while she rests.

In Your Community

People in your **community** notice when you are considerate of others. You can hold the door open for people.

Using good **manners** is a way to show you are considerate. Say "please" and "thank you" to someone who helps you in a store.

Anthony Leanna

Considerate people help others. Anthony Leanna had seen people in the hospital who had lost their hair from **cancer** treatment. He wanted to help them. Anthony started Heavenly Hats. His group sends new hats to people with cancer.

Fact!
Since 2001, Anthony has sent more than 35,000 hats to people with cancer.

C. S. Lewis

Author C. S. Lewis wrote many children's books. Young writers from around the world wrote letters to him. They asked his **advice** about writing. Lewis wrote back to everyone. He showed consideration for their thoughts and feelings.

Fact!
Children around the world enjoy C. S. Lewis' series of seven books, *The Chronicles of Narnia*.

What Would You Do?

Lexi's basketball team beat her friend Renata's team. Lexi is happy about winning. She wants to jump around. But Renata is sad. How can Lexi be considerate of Renata's feelings and still be happy about winning?

Fact!
A considerate athlete is called a good sport.

Amazing but True!

Volunteering is a way to show consideration for other people. Each year, more than 3 million people volunteer with the Salvation Army. Some of these volunteers serve at least 55 million free meals to people in need every year.

Hands On: Give Thank-You Notes

A good way to be considerate is to thank people when they are kind to you. You can give them thank-you notes.

What You Need

paper
pencil or pen
markers or crayons

What You Do

1. Think of something nice someone has done for you. Maybe someone gave you a gift. Maybe a friend helped you with your homework.
2. Write a note to that person. Thank him or her for being kind.
3. Decorate your note with markers or crayons.
4. Give your thank-you note to the person who was kind.

Glossary

advice (ad-VICE)—a suggestion about what someone should do

cancer (KAN-sur)—a disease in which cells in the body grow faster than normal and destroy healthy organs and tissues

community (kuh-MYOO-nuh-tee)—a group of people who live in the same area

example (eg-ZAM-puhl)—a model for others to follow

manners (MAN-urss)—polite behavior; people who use good manners are kind to other people.

Read More

Doudna, Kelly. *Thank You.* Good Manners. Edina, Minn.: Abdo, 2001.

Nettleton, Pamela Hill. *You First!: Kids Talk About Consideration.* Kids Talk. Minneapolis: Picture Window Books, 2005.

Raatma, Lucia. *Consideration.* Character Education. Mankato, Minn.: Bridgestone Books, 2000.

Internet Sites

FactHound offers a safe, fun way to find Internet sites related to this book. All of the sites on FactHound have been researched by our staff.

Here's how:

1. Visit *www.facthound.com*
2. Type in this special code **0736836772** for age-appropriate sites. Or enter a search word related to this book for a more general search.
3. Click on the **Fetch It** button.

FactHound will fetch the best sites for you!

Index

advice, 16
ask, 16

cancer, 14
care, 8
classmates, 4, 7
community, 12

example, 7

family, 10
feelings, 4, 16, 18
friends, 8–9, 18

games, 9, 18

Heavenly Hats, 14
help, 7, 10, 13, 14
homes, 8, 9, 10

invite, 8, 9

Leanna, Anthony, 14
Lewis, C. S., 16

manners, 13

needs, 10

people, 4, 10, 12, 14, 20

school, 4, 7
store, 13

teacher, 4, 7
thank, 9, 13
think, 4, 10

volunteer, 20